the
money coach

THE GOOD LIFE
MONEY MINDSET

8 Principles for Living
the Good Life Now

WORKBOOK

Exercises to learn how to develop new financial behaviors and habits to live a more confident, hopeful, and abundant life.

BARBARA D. WELCH, M.S

ISBN: 979-8-39591-257-2

CMG Publishing, LLC

Contents

Author's Note

CAN EVERYONE LIVE THE GOOD LIFE—a life that reflects their values and dreams? I say, yes! By becoming financially educated and by gaining the know-how, skills, and mindsets to manage our money, we can all enjoy successful lives.

When I started my financial career as a banker over 25 years ago, I noticed that many professionals, including myself, regardless of our areas of expertise, lacked financial savvy—the ability to successfully manage our finances. As I learned and became a financial expert, I shared that knowledge with my customers, my colleagues, and my community through presentations, workshops, and one-on-one coaching.

This workbook is made to accompany the "The Good Life Money Coach™" course, "The Good Life Money Mindset: 8 Principles For Living The Good Life Now". To participate in the course that coincides with this workbook, please visit the website at thegoodlifemoneycoach. com.

Introduction

AFTER MY HUSBAND AND I EXPERIENCED a devastating business failure in the late 90's and we began to rebuild our financial life, I learned that behavior dictates how you handle your finances. If you can learn how to master your behavior, you'll have the POWER to live THE GOOD LIFE!

If you want to live the good life, you've got to establish the right mindset before you can master the skills, strategies, and knowledge needed to manage your personal finances. So, before we jump head-first into the technical skills and strategies of money management, we will lay a foundation based on the reality that managing your money is more about how you behave than about what you know.

Your behavior is the result of your mindset. Your mindset is comprised of the values, beliefs, thoughts, feelings, and operating rules that influence your behavior, which, in turn, determine your results. So, if your current mindset is not getting you the results you want, no worries! Mindsets are not set in stone; our thoughts can be reset or renewed to form new behaviors and habits that produce the results we want.

The foundation that we are laying is built on the GOOD LIFE principles—eight principles that spell the acrostic: GOOD LIFE.

We'll cover these principles during the lessons in the course and practice them using the exercises in this workbook. We will continue to build upon them, reference them, and reinforce them in future classes, where we will dive into the money management skills, strategies, and knowledge necessary for success.

Here's to the good life money mindset!

the**good**life
money coach™
it's your life, make it good!™

Overview of the Course

The Good Life Money Mindset: 8 Principles for Living the Good Life Now

Overview Objectives

1. Describe and recall the GOOD LIFE principles.
2. Appraise your life against the GOOD LIFE principles.
3. Assess your personal values.
4. Develop goals around finance

Learning Tips and Housekeeping

The Good Life Money Coach™ Class offers a safe environment, meaning it has been designed to be respectful to and supportive of all participants as you learn and grow. You are invited and encouraged to be honest in your responses to help ensure you see growth throughout this class.

Let's go!

Five tips to help you get the most out of your Good Life Money Coach Workbook:

1. Schedule a specific time with reminders to complete each lesson of the class. Self-paced learning is a wonderful thing, but it is not uncommon to procrastinate when there are no deadlines.

2. Confirm your internet access, so you don't lose precious time with issues such as incorrectly assuming the coffee shop you've been wanting to work from has free Wi-Fi access.

3. Create a study space that offers you a quiet, clutter-free environment without distractions, which includes turning off your phone notifications.

4. Take brain and body breaks every 45 minutes to stay refreshed and focused. Stretch, breathe deeply, and let your mind wander for a few minutes. (No scrolling through your social media account!)

5. Take notes, journal, and highlight information to stay engaged and to capture the details that stand out to you. We've all found ourselves searching for that great insight that we forgot to write down!

   Writing is a psycho-neuro-motor activity. The act of writing forces you to think and concentrate. When you write your ideas, thoughts, and goals down in this workbook, you impress them into your subconscious mind, which then goes to work 24 hours a day to bring your goals to reality (Tracie).

Use these tips and you will have an enjoyable learning experience! Now, that you're all set to begin, let's get started.

Let's go!

Please watch the Welcome Video in the course.

Welcome to The Good Life Money Coach™. As I just shared in the welcome video, I will be your coach and your facilitator along your journey to find more satisfaction and success with your financial life. Let's jump right in with the class overview.

Upon completion of the class, you will be able to:

1. Describe and recall the GOOD LIFE principles.
2. Appraise your life against the GOOD LIFE principles.
3. Explain the elements—financial knowledge, mindsets, and behaviors—required for financial success.
4. Assess personal values/beliefs and observe how they impact your life (or observe how you are experiencing them).
5. Examine lifestyle habits that prevent the GOOD LIFE.
6. Develop goals around financial success and your ideal lifestyle.
7. Apply new tools and strategies around financial success and your ideal lifestyle.
8. Demonstrate the impact of the GOOD LIFE principles.

Just because you espouse a value does not mean it is evidenced in your life. By learning new behaviors, mindsets, and habits, you can begin to truly live your values and to bring those values out of the *future* and into the *present*. To help you along your journey, I will be sharing a little bit about my journey to GOOD LIFE living.

I prioritized my personal goals to be on the same level as my professional goals. I shifted my financial behaviors to better align with my core values of integrity, freedom, family, friends, and good health and to help me in pursuing my interests and in maintaining an overall sense of wellbeing.

Finally, I created an eight-point acrostic for the GOOD LIFE, and I live my life according to these eight principles. They have assisted me in seeing past money-myths, such as the scarcity myth or the ideas that money is evil or that working hard and struggling lead to success. They have also helped me to maintain the priorities I set and to see the power of gratitude and generosity.

That's a little bit more about my story. Now it's time to share your story in our introductory activity!

Introductory Activity:

Take 3-5 minutes to answer each of the following questions below, and then we'll get into the GOOD LIFE principles!

1. Write down your top 5 values. In other words, what is most important to you in life?

_____

_____

_____

_____

2. Describe what the good life would look like for you if you had no financial limits.

_____

_____

_____

_____

3. What objections came up as you were describing your good life? Take the time to acknowledge them by writing them down. This is an important step as you progress through the class.

_____

_____

_____

_____

The 8 Principles of the GOOD LIFE

Gratitude and Generosity — Gratitude is the simple, yet powerful, practice of showing appreciation, and it helps you focus on what is most important in life. Generosity is about being other-centered vs. self-centered, as well as maintaining an abundance mindset rather than a scarcity mindset. Practicing generosity boosts your sense of wellbeing.

Open Up to Accountability — This is the principle of being responsible to the people, plans, systems, and strategies that improve your financial life.

Operate According to a Detailed Financial Plan — Create a plan based on the 5 financial-planning areas to act as a guide and as a reminder of your goals as you work toward achieving financial success.

Discipline as a Way of Life — Discipline is a way of life for all of us. It is a mindset that is vital for a successful and good life.

Learn for a Lifetime — Be a lifelong learner—read, seek out opinions from experts, and develop and grow, both personally and professionally.

Invest in yourself — Invest in yourself, now and for the future, because you're worth it! Invest financially, physically, emotionally, mentally, spiritually, and occupationally.

Financial Freedom — Financial freedom is about enjoying life *now* by overcoming self-defeating beliefs and negative behaviors around money.

Examine the Good Life Stealers in Your Life — Examine your life for obstacles that lie between you and the life that you want. Look for the good-life-stealers in your life, which are any behaviors, habits, attitudes, or self-limiting beliefs that stop you from taking control of your life.

The Key is BELIEVING you can become what you dream to become through an intentional process of reprogramming your thinking. — Dr. Caroline Leaf

Find the "8 Principles Overview" video in the online course.

Lesson 1

Gratitude and Generosity

Lesson Introduction and Objectives

Hello and welcome to Lesson 1: Gratitude and Generosity. Now that you've completed the overview, including the introduction to the GOOD LIFE principles, we will discuss each of the principles in detail, starting with Generosity and Gratitude.

In this lesson, you will:

1. Express the benefits and the value of practicing gratitude and generosity.
2. Examine how gratitude and generosity are practiced as behaviors in your lifestyle.
3. Practice using tools that promote daily acts of gratitude and generosity.
4. Recognize the inextricable link between mindset and happiness.

Gratitude and Generosity Questionnaire:

In the course you *completed the Gratitude and Generosity Questionnaire.*

Takeaway: You can improve your wellbeing and your life satisfaction by increasing your levels of gratitude and generosity and by improving your financial situation.

After completing the questionnaire and examining our results, we now understand that we can all benefit from having more gratitude and generosity in our lives. Let's discuss what we mean by *gratitude* and *generosity.*

Gratitude

Gratitude is the quality of being thankful and returning kindness. It allows you to recognize and appreciate the things and people around you, regardless of your current life circumstances. Being grateful gives you a sense of wellbeing, a sense that your life has meaning, and the feeling that you are living your life to the fullest.

Research has shown that practicing gratitude has wide-ranging benefits, including increasing our happiness and resiliency levels, improving our health, and enhancing our relationships. Multiple studies have revealed the link between gratitude and wellbeing (Wood, Froh, & Geraghty, 2010).

When we are grateful, we tend to broaden our mindsets and to acknowledge, among other aspects, the roles that others play in our lives. Similarly, gratitude helps build durable mental resources related to wellbeing, such as intrinsic motivation and feelings of purposefulness (Froh & Bono, 2008). Specifically, gratitude is more than just a positive emotion because it also involves acknowledging and appreciating that one is a recipient of good things in life.

Other benefits of gratitude include:

- Increased longevity
- Increased imagination
- Increased resilience during life transitions, and
- Increased ability to solve problems (Leaf 2020; Wood et al., 2010).

It can be difficult to practice gratitude when you are struggling with your finances. You may feel envious of others and wish you could be more like them. If you lack gratitude, you fail to see all the wonderful people, experiences, and emotions in your own life. You overlook joy and disregard fun, believing others have what you think you are lacking.

Based on the research, the best way to cultivate a joyful life is to practice gratitude.

Practicing gratitude increases the level of dopamine—a feel-good hormone—in your brain and encourages your brain to seek more of the same. Scientifically speaking, the more gratitude you have in your life, the more you will find.

A gratitude-based mindset will come with daily practice. Not only does the research support this idea, but I have also found it to be true in my own life.

Activity:

Please complete the following activity by sharing your thoughts below.

Read the handout "How to Practice Gratitude," which is based on "9 Ways To Cultivate Joy With Gratitude" (Livelytable.com) and "The 5-Minute Gratitude Journal" by Sophia Godkin, PhD, which can be found in the online course.

1. After reading the handout, please take 5 minutes to journal about your takeaways from the handout.

_____

_____

_____

_____

Reflection Activity:

Please complete the following activity by sharing your thoughts below.

1. Recall a time you showed appreciation to others:

_____

_____

_____

_____

2. Recall a time when your focus was on what you have vs. what you don't have:

_____

_____

_____

_____

Generosity

Generosity is the quality of being kind and generous. It has been defined as going beyond what is expected of you. But what does this have to do with your money? Well, studies offer evidence of this simple act's ability to insulate you from greed (known to end in debt, financial ruin, or worse) and to enhance your happiness and wellbeing. It is simple yet powerful to serve others.

Greed or avarice is defined as excessive or insatiable desire for wealth or gain, and is one of those things that is hard to see in yourself. I've never met a person that thinks that they are greedy, but we all have greed for something—it is human nature. Recognize it and what it says about yourself and your life rather than righteously rejecting or denying it.

Here are some examples of the way greed shows up:

Never Having Enough & Discontentment

There seems to be no limit on what 'enough' entails. This is a slippery slope that can lead to poverty or worse. A salary of $37,000 is more than 96% of the world's population. So, if you earn more than that, you are in the top 4% of wage earners in the world! Research shows that after about middle-class status, there is little additional happiness to gain from material possessions.

Overindulging

The bad habits of overeating and excessive drinking can lead to obesity and alcoholism, both of which are costly to your physical and financial health. An obese adult spends 42% more on healthcare than someone with a healthy weight. In the United States, obesity accounts for $210 billion in healthcare costs, and this does not take into consideration the loss of quality of life. Alcoholism or other substance abuse disorders commonly lead to physical and mental health issues.

Of course, there are other ways to overindulge, such as over-spending on cars, housing, clothes, or entertainment. The average American's debt (per U.S. adult) is $58,604, and 77% of American households have at least one type of debt.

Recovering from overindulging can be costly. And there are the other problems stemming from excessive lifestyles, including time taken off work, a lack of drive or motivation, and the sheer expense of maintaining these habits.

Selfishness

Unhealthy selfishness, unlike spiritual selfishness, which centers around, attunes to, acknowledges, and honors the needs of the self, is a form of greed and appears in many ways, such as hoarding possessions, never giving to charity, penny-pinching, and stockpiling wealth. Selfishness kills your joy, sets unrealistic expectations, and strains relationships. Selfishness can ruin your life if you let it take over, but it doesn't have to.

Gambling

Gambling is the practice or activity of betting—the practice of risking money or other stakes in a game or bet. Gambling can quickly go from a fun, harmless diversion to an unhealthy or compulsive obsession with serious consequences. Whether it's betting on sports, scratch cards, roulette, poker, or slots—in a casino, at the track, or online—a gambling problem can strain relationships, interfere with work, and lead to financial disaster. A person might run up huge debts or even steal money to gamble.

The biggest step to overcoming a gambling addiction is realizing that there is a problem. It takes tremendous strength and courage to own up to this, but it is possible with the right support, such as joining Gamblers Anonymous or seeing a therapist.

My Journey to Generosity

When I began the good life journey years ago, I hadn't really given much thought to the benefits associated with generosity or giving—whether it was volunteering my time, giving a thoughtful gift to someone, or just taking time to listen to someone in need of some encouragement and love, it was the right thing to do. I never really thought about how I felt about it until my husband and I began to experience some serious financial difficulties, and I came to the realization that it was going to take some time for us to work our way out of it.

I was stressed and fighting depression and self-pity, but I found that, as I practiced generosity, I focused on others instead of being so self-centered and self-absorbed with my financial problems, and I felt better!

Research on kindness shows that being generous decreases your stress levels (Fryburg, 2021). Kindness is free, widely available, and has no side effects. It generates a response in your brain by increasing oxytocin, which makes us feel connected to and trusting of others. It protects your cardiovascular system—your heart— and strengthens your immune system, and it improves your energy, confidence, and longevity! Another important neurotransmitter affected by kindness is serotonin, which is great for reducing anxiety, relieving depression, and increasing happiness. Endorphins are also released, giving you a "helper's high" (Dossey L. 2018).

The thing is, sometimes we need to step out of our situations. You may think if you continue to think about the problem and ruminate on it that a solution is going to come. However, ruminating is only going to make the situation worse.

When I started understanding and practicing generosity more intentionally, I realized that there are always people less fortunate than me and that misfortune is not just financial—it manifests in various ways. Someone who is doing well financially has other problems and other concerns in life. A simple act of kindness is fulfilling, giving you a sense of wellbeing and the hope that everything will be okay, in addition to all the health benefits.

This mindset shift is a win-win for everyone concerned. This simple change becomes a powerful principle that helps make life good!

Let's get real!

Activity:

Consider the following questions and write your answers below.

1. Recall a time you showed generosity by giving to or investing in someone else.

   _____

   _____

   _____

   _____

2. How have selfishness, greed, and materialism impacted you throughout your life?

   _____

   _____

   _____

   _____

3. Take a moment to recall a time when you gave into greed or materialism (for example, overpaying or spending outside of your means, disregarding the feelings of others, sacrificing your wellbeing for personal gain, never giving to charity, penny-pinching, or stockpiling).

   _____

   _____

   _____

   _____

How to Practice Generosity

The practice of generosity protects you from the effects of greed, as you become more other-centered and appreciative of what you have.

Give Forgiveness

Forgiveness means different things to different people. However, it generally involves a decision to let go of resentment and thoughts of revenge. The act that hurt or offended you might always be with you, but forgiveness can lessen its grip on you and help free you from the control of the person who harmed you. For more information on how to forgive go to class resources.

Perform Acts of Kindness

This means giving more than what is expected of you. An example of an act of kindness might be when your friend takes the couch and lets you sleep in their bed when you stay over at her place. She didn't have to do that. Or it might look like going the extra mile to help a customer, client, or team member at work.

Let's get real!

Activity:

Please complete the following activity by practicing the prompts below.

Start small — Try 3–5 acts of kindness per week. Ask yourself, "Who around me could use a little kindness?" You might carry someone's groceries, hold open a door for someone behind you, or send a quick appreciative note to a family member, a friend, a coworker, or an acquaintance.

Get Inspired — Watch Botlhate Tshetlo's TED talk about her decision to complete 38 acts of kindness to celebrate her 38th birthday (see class resources: My 38 random acts of kindness: Botlhale Tshetlo at TEDxSoweto 2013).

Learn About Health Benefits — Listen to this podcast from University Hospitals: The 'Science Behind Kindness and How It Benefits Your Health (sounddiscipline.org).

Give Grace — Don't judge people. Give people's behavior the most generous explanation you can think of.

Give Time, Talent, and Treasure — Give your time, talent, and treasure to people and causes you care about. A collaborative study by University of British Columbia researchers, Elizabeth Dunn and Lara Akinand, and Michael Norton of Harvard Business School showed that spending as little as $5 a day on someone else can significantly boost happiness (Julie Ann Caitns, 2015).

Reflection Activity:

Consider the following questions and write your answers below.

1. Think and write briefly about a time that you gave to someone else. How did it make you feel?

_____

_____

_____

_____

_____

2. Can you recall a boost of happiness in that moment? Write about that happy moment.

_____

_____

_____

_____

Take a moment to watch this fifteen-minute TED Talk video: "Helping others makes us happier -- but it matters how we do it | Elizabeth Dunn." (Find the video in course resources or online on YouTube).

Summary:

Gratitude and generosity are crucial for the good life money mindset. Gratitude, if you recall, is the quality of being thankful and returning kindness, and gratitude is the quality of being kind and giving.

Researchers have found that both gratitude and generosity have a strong positive impact on a person's sense of wellbeing, while opposing traits, such as greed, have negative consequences.

Practicing gratitude and generosity in your everyday life can help boost your mood and sense of wellbeing, which, in turn, will help you to achieve your good life!

Lesson Recap:

1. In this lesson I was able to: (check all that apply)

   ☐ Express the benefits/value of practicing generosity & gratitude.
   ☐ Examine how generosity & gratitude are practiced in my current lifestyle.

- Practice using tools that promote daily acts of generosity & gratitude.
- Recognize the inextricable link between mindset and happiness.

2. How do you feel about this course after this lesson? Do you feel confident in practicing generosity & gratitude? Why or why not?

_____

_____

_____

_____

_____

3. What is something you appreciated about this lesson? What would you change? Do you have feedback for the instructor?

_____

_____

_____

_____

_____

*Merriam-webster.com

Lesson 2

Open Up to Accountability

Lesson Introduction and Objectives

In this lesson, we will focus on Opening up to Accountability.

In this lesson, you will:

1. Recognize the benefit & value of accountability.
2. Discuss your current financial accountability.
3. Discover new tools and strategies for financial accountability.

Accountability

Accountability is about taking responsibility for your life and doing whatever is required to follow through on expectations and commitments, which can feel overwhelming when it comes to managing every area of your finances (covered in the next lesson). For now, you can breathe easy, knowing that you don't have to do it alone. None of us know it all, but by being open and accountable to supportive and qualified partnerships and by taking advantage of the right systems, strategies, and tools, you'll be on top of your responsibility game in no time!

In short, open up to accountability to people, plans, systems, and strategies. Let's start with People.

People — Find a seasoned financial planner, accountant, tax preparer, personal assistant, friend, coach, or therapist. Working with an accountability partner is a key to success for anyone who wants to change and grow.

Plans — Plans help you set goals and keep deadlines. Develop a spending plan, AKA a budget, using an app, a digital spreadsheet, or the tried and true "old school" pad of paper. There are other financial plans you'll also need to develop, such as short- and long-term saving & investing plans, retirement, and tax and estate planning—but we'll talk more about plans in the next lesson.

Systems and Strategies — Systems and strategies help you organize and accomplish your goals. Some examples include: bill organization and recordkeeping, bill payment, debt payoff systems and strategies, systems for making purchasing decisions, and strategies for maximizing your income.

Benefits of Accountability

1. Accomplishing Goals — Being accountable to others offers the support and encouragement to get things done as planned!

2. Activating Honor — We all want to be recognized as a person who can be trusted to keep our word to ourselves and to others, and it feels great to follow through on our commitments.

3. Improving Results and Performance — By setting goals and by measuring your performance towards achieving those goals, you can recognize your success sooner.

4. Gaining Knowledge and Experience — By investing in the right people, plans, and systems, you benefit from dependable knowledge and experience that you can trust.

Let's get real!

Activity:

Please complete the following two questions by filling in the blank spaces.

1. Opening up to Accountability is about _____

    _____

    _____

    _____

2. Being open and accountable to _____ and _____
    partnerships and taking advantage of the right _____,
    _____, and _____.

Answers:

1. Opening up to Accountability is about taking responsibility for your life and doing whatever is required to follow through on expectations and commitments.

2. Being open and accountable to supportive and qualified partnerships and by taking advantage of the right systems, strategies, and tools.

Tools and Strategies for Developing and Improving Financial Accountability

1. Create a plan for developing the areas of accountability and improving the behaviors identified in the last question and track your progress using the GOOD LIFE Behaviors Practice Plan™ (see Lesson 8).

2. Celebrate your wins, whether small or large, daily to remain motivated to achieve your goal.

3. Incentivize your progress by rewarding yourself with a small pleasure. Perhaps it's checking off your accomplishments each

day, or it's treating yourself to an experience or item when you stay on track or reach a goal after a month.

4. Find an accountability partner. This person should be someone you trust—ideally, someone who has similar goals or a shared perspective on success and growth. If you haven't already, plan to join the accountability community for this class.

5. View everyday as a fresh start. The fresh-start effect will boost your motivation. Examples of the fresh-start effect are creating a fresh checklist, forgiving yourself for a bad day, or downloading a new app that will help you achieve your goal (Dai, H., Milkman, K.L., & Riis, J. 2014).

Let's get real!

Reflection Activity:

Please complete the following reflection activity.

Recall: After watching the video in the course, you were asked to select the areas of accountability that you would like to improve, as well as which accountability benefit resonates with you the most.

Areas of Accountability

☐ People
☐ Plans
☐ Systems and Strategies

Accountability Benefits

☐ Accomplish Goals
☐ Activate Honor
☐ Improve results and performance
☐ Gain knowledge and experience

1. Take a few minutes to journal about why you selected the area(s) of accountability that you did. Be honest and thoughtful as you write. Remember, writing forces you to think and to concentrate. To change your mindset, you must consciously acknowledge what you want to change so that these new ideas enter your subconscious mind. Once the subconscious mind accepts an idea, it begins to execute it (Murphy, J. The Power of Your Subconscious Mind).

_____

_____

_____

_____

2. Next, journal about why you selected the accountability benefit(s). Again, be honest and thoughtful as you write. This will help you as you create a plan later in the course.

_____

_____

_____

_____

3. Now, journal about the behaviors you identified in the course that you need to improve. Why do you need or want to improve these behaviors?

Accountability Behaviors

- [ ] Being trustworthy
- [ ] Following through
- [ ] Setting deadlines and goals

- ☐ Reporting and or measuring your performance
- ☐ Making responsible decisions
- ☐ Establishing and maintaining positive relationships

_____

_____

_____

_____

Summary:

Open up to accountability by taking responsibility for your life and by doing whatever is necessary to follow through on your commitments and goals. The benefits of accountability include accomplishing your goals, experiencing feelings of honor, improving your results and performance, and gaining knowledge and experience. You can develop your accountability skills by creating plans, by incentivizing and celebrating your progress, and by finding an accountability partner.

If you hold yourself accountable to people, plans, and systems and strategies, you will quickly experience the wonderful benefits of accountability and move one step closer to living your good life!

Lesson Recap:

1. In this lesson I was able to: (check all that apply)

   - ☐ Recognize the benefit & value of accountability
   - ☐ Consider my current financial accountability
   - ☐ Discover new tools and strategies for financial accountability

2. How do you feel about this course after this lesson? Do you feel confident in opening up to accountability? Why or why not?

_____

_____

_____

_____

_____

3. What is something you appreciated about this lesson? What would you change? Do you have feedback for the instructor?

_____

_____

_____

_____

Lesson 3

Operate According to a Detailed Financial Plan

Lesson Introduction and Objectives

As mentioned in the previous lesson on accountability to people, plans, and processes, this lesson will focus on creating a plan and on operating according to a detailed financial plan.

In this lesson, you will:

1. Name the 6 areas of a financial plan.
2. Explain the benefits of operating according to a financial plan.
3. Identify and assess gaps in your current financial plan.

Detailed Financial Planning

A plan is a guide for, and a reminder of, your goals as you work to achieve them. A financial plan should cover six areas, which I share here in an easy-to-remember acrostic: BRIITE.

Basics
Retirement
Investments & Savings
Insurance
Tax
Estate

Basics

The Basics refer to a general spending plan or budget, managing checking and savings accounts, credit scores, and debt management.

Retirement

Retirement includes investing now to replace your income when you don't want to work anymore. Research shows that you will need 70% to 90% of your pre-retirement income to maintain your current standard of living. IRAs, company-sponsored 401(k)s, and 403(b)'s are the most popular vehicles for saving for retirement (Bearden,2022).

Investments and Savings

Investment and savings accounts are tools used to help you accumulate money for your financial goals. They both pay interest on the money deposited based on the type of account and its risk level, which ranges from the low-risk guaranteed interest rate of a savings account to the high-risk, high-return potential of a company stock.

We'll cover savings and investments in more detail in future classes, but for now here's a little more introductory information on investments and savings.

It's important to be both a saver and an investor. Savings accounts are best for accumulating money that you need for short-term goals (0–5 years) and for emergency needs that could occur at any time, such as a loss of income, major car repairs, insurance deductibles, and other unexpected expenses. The current average savings rate at the printing of this workbook is .05% to 3%.

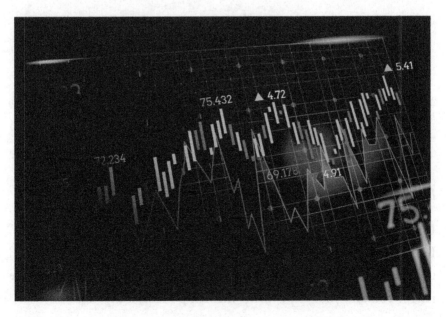

Investments such as stocks, bonds, and mutual funds are best for long-term financial goals (7 years or more), and they should use money that is not needed for short-term goals or regular living expenses. Examples of long-term investment goals include funding college expenses, saving for retirement, starting a business, or purchasing real estate. Historically, the stock market has offered a return of 9–10% over a 7-year period.

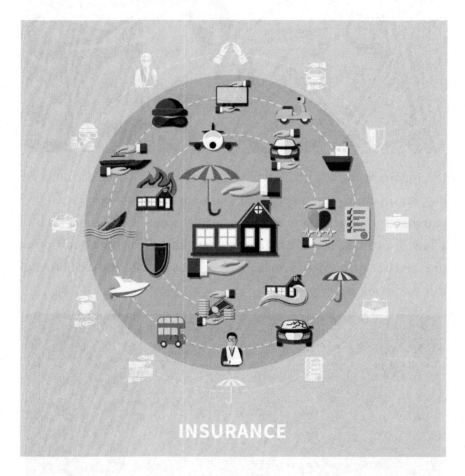

INSURANCE

Insurance Planning

Life, health, and property insurances protect you against financial loss. Life insurance offers an instant estate to dependents of the insured in the event of death. Health insurance or medical insurance covers the risk of you and your dependents incurring medical expenses.

Meanwhile, property insurance includes home and car coverage covers the risk of damage or theft to your home or vehicle.

Tax Planning

No one wants to pay taxes, but being in a higher tax bracket means you're earning more money. Tax planning offers strategies to help reduce and/or eliminate taxes—either now or in the future. Examples of tax planning include using Roth or Traditional IRA's (Individual Retirement Accounts) or investing in an employer sponsored 401k or 403b retirement account, which allow you to accumulate money and interest tax free or defer paying income tax until the age required by the IRS for required minimum distributions (RMD), which is 72 or 73 (if you reach age 72 after Dec. 31, 2022). Note that Roth IRA's are funded with post tax dollars. We'll cover retirement planning accounts in depth in future courses.

Estate Planning

For most people, the good life includes being able to take care of their loved ones, especially their dependents, by leaving a financial legacy for the next generation to build upon. When individuals do not leave their estates in order, they rob the next generation of financial opportunities because those living family members will have to cover the expenses of the deceased individual. End-of-life costs are very expensive. Not only must the funeral or memorial service be funded, but also, when wills and medical directives are not in place, it can mean heirs may incur additional legal expenses to claim possession of any assets.

Leaving your loved ones to handle your affairs—affairs that you are responsible for and can best handle—is an act of love. In Lesson 1, we learned the first principle of living the good life is practicing gratitude and generosity. Generosity is when we are selfless and when we think of others. It is selfless to face the reality of the end of our lives and to take steps to get our affairs in order. It's best to start estate planning as a young adult and to review it every few years. There's a whole lot of life to enjoy in between those review meetings, including the peace of mind and the satisfaction that you have done the right thing to ensure that the assets you have worked for all your life are passed on to your family.

I learned that to live the good life, having a spending plan (aka: a budget), a cash reserve savings account, a retirement plan, insurance, or an estate plan, which includes a trust, a last will and testament, and a medical directive protects your finances.

For instance, a retirement plan prepares you for the future when you do not want to "have to" work every day and you want both flexibility and financial independence. Having a retirement income gives you financial freedom—another GOOD LIFE principle discussed in Lesson 7. When you operate according to a detailed financial plan, you are able to plan for the things and experiences you want during your lifetime.

Personally, I found great satisfaction once I understood the importance of having a detailed financial plan. My family and I enjoyed the security, the stability, and the peace of mind of knowing that things were in order—that we had a system, tools, and products in place that offered us the foundation and framework to build and live the good life.

Benefits of Operating According to a Detailed Financial Plan

1. It offers best practice approaches to save, spend, invest, and protect your earnings.

2. It gives you direction and assurance that you are working toward achieving your financial goals.

3. It acts as a guide and offers proof that you are moving toward your goals—it is a tangible symbol of your hard work.

4. It helps you maintain control of your income, expenses, and investments, so you can achieve your goals.

5. It provides financial security for you and your family.

6. It creates peace of mind.

Let's get real!

Activity:

Please complete the following activity by sharing your thoughts below.

1. Select the top 2 benefits from the list above that resonate with you the most and take a few minutes to journal about why they resonate. Remember to be honest and thoughtful as you write.

_____

_____

_____

_____

Activity:

Please complete the following activity.

Recall: After watching the video in the course, you were asked to complete the following checklist.

Assessing Your Current Financial Plan:

- ☐ You know how much you owe.
- ☐ You have easy access to your debt amounts.
- ☐ All your accounts are in good standing.
- ☐ You have life, health, and property insurance in place to protect your finances.
- ☐ You have a will and a trust in place.
- ☐ You are saving a portion of your income on a consistent basis.

- ☐ You are investing in a retirement plan.
- ☐ You can increase your income or cut your spending.
- ☐ You have a plan to pay any outstanding debt.

If any of these signs apply to you, congratulations! You have the right mindset to get your finances in shape!

Reflection Activity:

Please complete the following reflection activity by answering the questions below.

Imagine that you have a financial plan in place that includes the financial planning areas (BRIITE) and assumes that you are maximizing your ability to spend, save, invest, and protect your earnings.

1. Describe how you feel in detail. How do you feel physically, emotionally, mentally? What does this mean to you? What can you do now that this plan is in place?

_____

_____

_____

_____

2. What did you do to put this plan into place? Remember, you are imagining what you did to put this plan into place, even if the plan is not currently in place.

_____

_____

_____

Summary:

To achieve the good life money mindset, you need to create and operate according to a detailed financial plan. A detailed financial plan covers six areas: *Basics, Retirement, Investments & Savings, Insurance, Tax*, and *Estate planning*, or **BRIITE**.

Operating according to a detailed financial plan results in numerous benefits, such as protection for your earnings and assets, direction, and guidance for achieving your financial goals, and the comfort of knowing you and your family have achieved financial security and are on the path toward living your good life!

Lesson Recap:

1. In this lesson I was able to: (check all that apply)

   ☐ Name the 6 areas of a financial plan.
   ☐ Explain the benefits of operating according to a financial plan.
   ☐ Identify and assess gaps in your current financial plan.

2. How do you feel about this course after this lesson? Do you understand the importance of operating according to a financial plan? Why or why not?

_____

_____

_____

_____

3. What is something you appreciated about this lesson? What would you change? Do you have feedback for the instructor?

_____

_____

_____

_____

_____

Lesson 4

Discipline as a Way of Life

Lesson Introduction and Objectives

In the last lesson, we discussed the areas included in a detailed financial plan and how plans contribute to financial success. Along with detailed planning, financial success requires discipline. In this lesson we will delve into discipline as a way of life!

In this lesson you will:

1. Define self-discipline and explain its importance
2. Rate your level of self-discipline.
3. Identify strategies to build better self-discipline.
4. Complete a two-week challenge focused on discipline.

Discipline

Discipline is a way of life for all of us. It is a mindset that is vital for a successful and good life. Discipline as a way of life begins in childhood, during which time we learn social skills and self-control.

Discipline is defined as action or inaction that is regulated to be in accordance with a particular system of governance or management. It can also be defined as controlling one's own behavior for a specific outcome or goal using self-control, motivation, persistence, and goals.

When you have discipline, you can focus and complete tasks, no matter the circumstances.

Let's get real!

Activity:

Please complete the following activity by sharing your thoughts below.

In the course, I provided you with three examples of financial goals and the controlling or disciplined actions required to achieve those goals. Now it's your turn!

1. Write down one financial goal that you have.

_____

_____

_____

_____

2. Write down the controlling or disciplined action required of you to achieve your goal.

_____

_____

_____

_____

Self-Assessment:

Please complete the following self-assessment by selecting the response which best represents your feelings.

1. On a scale of 1–10 with 1 representing not disciplined and 10 representing completely disciplined, how would you rate your overall level of self-discipline?

   1   2   3   4   5   6   7   8   9   10

For questions 2–11, please use the following table to guide your answers.

All the time	4
Most of the time	3
Occasionally	2
Never	1

2. Discipline — I am able to focus and complete tasks no matter the circumstances.

   1   2   3   4

3. Self-Control — I am able to control my desires, moods, actions, emotions, words, and personal focus.

   1   2   3   4

4. Motivation — I am able to take initiative to encourage myself to keep achieving my goals.

   1   2   3   4

5. Persistence & Commitment — I am able to overcome failure and still continue on the path to success.

   1   2   3   4

6. Goals — I am able to set goals and see tangible success and achievements in my life.

1	2	3	4

7. Ambition — I have the desire and determination to achieve my dreams and desires.

1	2	3	4

8. Organization — I maintain an orderly environment at work and at home, meet due dates and deadlines, and communicate well with my family, friends, and co-workers.

1	2	3	4

9. Responsibility — I know what is expected of me at work and at home, and I deliver on those expectations.

1	2	3	4

10. Resilience — I am able to face and adapt to challenges, disappointments, and setbacks and to overcome them.

1	2	3	4

11. Work Ethic — I believe that hard work is fundamentally valuable and is worth pursuing, and I demonstrate this by consistently showing up prepared to deliver results.

1	2	3	4

Score and feedback:

51 - 54 — Impressive! You consistently demonstrate the behaviors needed for healthy self-discipline.

39 - 50 — Good job! You demonstrate the behaviors needed for healthy self-discipline most of the time.

22 - 38 — You are making an effort! You occasionally demonstrate the behaviors needed for healthy self-discipline.

11 - 21 — You are in the right place! You need to develop behaviors needed for healthy self-discipline

Self-Discipline and Financial Success

Self-discipline and financial success go hand-in-hand. Why is self-discipline important for financial success?

1. It helps you meet financial obligations, so you can maintain or improve your lifestyle.

2. It helps you reach your short- and long-term financial goals, so you can fund your needs and wants.

3. It helps you prepare for your future retirement goals, so you can relax when the time comes.

4. It helps you delay gratification or avoid temptation in the short-term, so you can stay focused on what's most important in the long-term.

5. It helps you learn to focus on and pay attention to your financial priorities without distraction, so you can maintain financial awareness.

As we consider strategies to become more financially disciplined, first consider how you are motivated to maintain discipline.

We are all motivated by positive and negative consequences; however, you may tend toward one or the other. The following exercise will help you to determine your personal motivation style.

Let's get real!

Reflective Activity:

Take a moment to consider whether you are more motivated by positive or negative consequences, then please complete the following reflective activity.

To complete this activity, select which statement best describes you.

1.

  a. You discipline yourself to show up to work on time because you need your job and because your employer can terminate you.

  OR

  b. You discipline yourself to show up to work on time because you respect yourself, you value your job and income, and your employer can promote you.

2.

  a. You discipline yourself to file a timely tax return because the IRS can garnish your pay or charge penalties and fees.

  OR

  b. You discipline yourself to file a timely tax return because the IRS can offer refunds, write-offs, and tax credits.

3.

  a. You discipline yourself to pay your mortgage or rent on time because the mortgage lender can foreclose on your property or the property manager can evict you and report your late payment to credit bureaus, resulting in a bad credit score.

  OR

  b. You discipline yourself to pay your mortgage or rent on time because you appreciate your home, and the mortgage lender or property manager can report your timely payment to credit bureaus, resulting in a good credit score.

4.

    a.   You discipline yourself to pay your car note on time because the lender can repossess your car and your credit will be bad.

        OR

    b.   You discipline yourself to pay your car note on time because you appreciate having transportation, you are motivated to pay if off, and it builds a positive credit score.

Results:

If most of your answers were (a): You tend to be motivated by negative consequences to maintain discipline.

If most of your answers were (b): You tend to be motivated by positive consequences to maintain discipline.

The Science of Motivation

In order to build self-discipline, we need to understand what happens emotionally and neurologically when we practice positive-consequence or negative-consequence discipline strategies.

When we are focused on positive consequences, endorphins are released that boost our moods. At the same time, healthy neural pathways are formed in our brains. The more we practice positive-consequence discipline, the more these actions become ingrained in our brains, until they become new habits.

Conversely, focusing on negative consequences causes anxiety, which releases adrenaline and cortisol, and which creates unhealthy neural pathways. These actions then become ingrained in our brains as habitual.

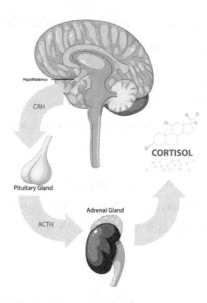

When we focus on positive consequences, it causes feelings of joy, happiness, or optimism, and serotonin is released. Serotonin is the "happy" hormone that improves your mood and creates a sense of wellbeing.

When we focus on negative consequences, it can lead to anxiety and depression, as the levels of cortisol and adrenaline are increased and as the levels of serotonin, dopamine—the "motivation and habit forming" chemical—and norepinephrine are reduced.

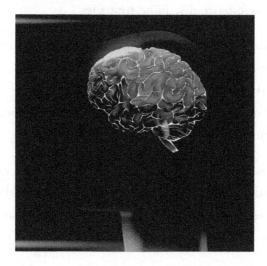

Strategies to Build Healthy Self-Discipline

Can you change and build healthy self-discipline skills? Of course! You do it every day, depending on your situations. However, permanent behavioral change comes only with awareness and practice.

Practice, practice, practice! Using the incredible power of our minds we can practice discipline to improve our lives. You can use the following strategies to help develop a healthy sense of self-discipline:

1. Identify areas of improvement by referencing the self-discipline assessment. Begin practicing and monitoring your progress on mastering these new mindsets and traits.

2. Practice sitting with discomfort or pressure. Discomfort or pressure can be positive (e.g., strenuous exercise that strengthens your muscles or sleepiness that signals you to rest your body). The tension between delayed and instant gratification is positive discomfort caused by your self-discipline muscle being stretched and strengthened.

3. Practice being comfortable taking calculated risks or stepping out on faith.

4. Practice being patient. Actively wait by controlling and doing EVERYTHING you can (like practicing the GOOD LIFE principles!), and don't forget to celebrate your small wins along the way.

5. Practice self-respect by showing respect for your goals and your plans for achieving them and by honoring your word to yourself.

6. Practice thinking and saying positive things about yourself, your plans, and your goals. What do you think and say about yourself when it comes to your finances?

GOOD LIFE discipline comes with consistently practicing new habits and mindsets to achieve your GOOD LIFE goals. To practice positive self-discipline, your assignment is to use these strategies to complete a two-week challenge to improve your self-discipline in a financial area of your choice.

Let's get real!

Activity:

Please complete the following activity by sharing your thoughts below.

1. Compare your financial goal to the top five values you identified in the "Introductory Activity." Write down your thoughts.

_____

_____

_____

_____

_____

Reflective Activity:

Please complete the reflective activity by sharing your thoughts below.

1. Review your top 5 values from lesson one and consider how self-discipline is needed to uphold your values. Write down your thoughts.

_____

_____

_____

_____

_____

Summary:

Discipline is a way of life for all of us. It is a mindset that is vital for a successful and good life. It can be defined as controlling behavior for a specific outcome or goal using self-control, motivation, persistence, and goals.

When you have discipline, you are able to focus and complete tasks, no matter the circumstances.

We are all motivated by positive and negative consequences, which, in turn, cause positive or negative feelings based on the chemicals released in our brains. Using the incredible power of our minds, we can practice discipline to improve our lives.

Lesson Recap:

1. In this lesson I was able to: (check all that apply.)

   ☐ Rate my level of self-discipline.
   ☐ Define self-discipline and explain its importance.
   ☐ Identify strategies to build better self-discipline.
   ☐ Complete a two-week challenge focused on discipline

2. How do you feel about this course after this lesson? Do you feel confident in integrating discipline as a way of life? Why or why not?

   _____

   _____

   _____

   _____

   _____

3. What is something you appreciated about this lesson? What would you change? Do you have feedback for the instructor?

   _____

   _____

   _____

   _____

   _____

Lesson 5

Learn for a Lifetime

Lesson Introduction and Objectives

In the last lesson, we discussed the importance of discipline in managing your finances. I hope you took me up on the 2-week challenge to help increase your level of discipline! In this lesson, we discover the importance of learning for a lifetime. L is for Learn for a Lifetime.

In this lesson you will:

1. Restate the benefits of being a lifelong learner.
2. Identify something you want to learn more about.

Lifelong Learning

Learning is a part of life and happens every day in a myriad of ways—from the informal, such as reading a book, trying a new recipe, or watching a how-to video, to the formal, such as going back to school or taking an online course, like this one!

Lifelong learning is an asset that you can give yourself at any age. Lifelong learning is a GOOD LIFE key that can unlock doors to new opportunities, offer access to new possibilities, and provide you with options for fulfilling your goals and dreams in every facet of life.

Benefits of Learning for a Lifetime

1. It can help you succeed in your career or job at any level.

    Additional education can help you achieve your career goals, like making more money, advancing in your current occupation, or starting in a different one. You'll gain knowledge, enhance your soft skills, and demonstrate a strong work ethic. A study by Oxford University found that when people study at a university or college, they tended to boost their agreeableness and likeability—both of which are a boon to forming positive relationships and getting ahead.

2. It can help you stay mentally sharp.

    Forming new connections between the neurons we've still got is how the aging brain keeps itself fresh and functioning optimally. According to Dr. Norman Doidge in his book, *The Brain That Changes Itself*, people who don't feed their brains by learning new things have been shown to suffer various types of mental atrophy, resulting in much higher rates of dementia and other cognitive functioning deficits in their senior years. On a more positive note, fascinating research at the University of California Davis also finds curiosity helps your brain remain more open to additional learning, and this openness helps you remember new information and cement memories.

3. It can help you connect to new people and ideas.

    Research shows that most people are likely to find connections with like-minded individuals who share similar interests. Engaging in lifelong learning can present opportunities to develop new relationships with other learners or to nurture existing connections by sharing or exchanging knowledge.

4. It can help you stay more fulfilled.

Feeling fulfilled includes feeling like there is always something more to learn. Being open to learning new skills or taking on a new project at work can it much easier to feel satisfied. The best way to feel fulfilled in life is through growth.

5. It can help you be happier, and happier people earn more money!

   As you learned in lesson one, research on happiness suggests happiness arises when we are generous, grateful, and connected with our people. But another lesser-known pathway toward happiness is learning, growing, and challenging ourselves in new ways. When you learn new things, you also expand your horizons, and that wider perspective is linked to experiences of happiness and joy.

> *Anyone who stops learning is old, whether at twenty or eighty. Anyone who keeps learning stays young. The greatest thing in life is to keep your mind young. — Henry Ford*

Let's get real!

Activity:

Please complete the following activity by sharing your thoughts below.

1. Identify something you would like to learn and start reaping the good life benefits of learning!

_____

_____

_____

_____

Reflective Activity:

Please complete the following Reflective Activity by answering the questions below.

1. What was your mindset about learning before and after the lesson?

_____

_____

_____

_____

2. What did you find most surprising about the benefits of learning?

_____

_____

_____

Summary:

Evidence of learning is demonstrated change. New behaviors and mindsets become inherent as you practice them habitually. Be curious, seek expanded knowledge, and never stop learning.

Lesson Recap:

1. In this lesson I was able to: (check all that apply)

   ☐ Restate the benefits being a lifelong learner.
   ☐ Identify something I want to learn more about.

2. How do you feel about this course after this lesson? Do you feel confident in implementing lifelong learning? Why or why not?

   _____

   _____

   _____

   _____

3. What is something you appreciated about this lesson? What would you change? Do you have feedback for the instructor?

   _____

   _____

   _____

   _____

Lesson 6

Invest in Yourself

Lesson Introduction and Objectives

In the last lesson, we discussed the importance of lifetime learning for living a good life. In this lesson we will continue to explore the ways you can improve your life—financially and otherwise—by investing in yourself.

In this lesson, you will:

1. Assess the various types of self-investment.
2. Explain the benefits of both current & long-term investment.
3. Recall the value of investing in yourself.

4. Assess the (first 5) GOOD LIFE principles for self-investment opportunities.

Investing in Yourself

Invest in yourself—now and for the future—because you're worth it! It is possible to enjoy the good life for a lifetime when you understand, value, and adopt a healthy mindset about investing in yourself, whether emotionally, mentally, physically, occupationally, and of course, financially. When you invest in each of these facets, they work synergistically, creating wellness in your life that helps propel you forward to achieve your life goals and to live your version of the good life.

Financial Self-Investment

Develop, implement, and maintain a plan to earn, save, invest, spend, and protect your finances to improve and maintain your lifestyle. Financial self-investment includes viewing saving, investing, and spending on needs or obligations as gifts to yourself and not as penalties.

Recall the lesson for the principle, Discipline as a Way of Life. We learned how our perspectives, whether positive or negative, affect our mindsets about money. Our thoughts create emotional and neurological responses, which form either an abundance or limited mindset. For example, if you view saving, investing, and spending on bills as gifts to yourself, you will experience an emotional response as mood-boosting hormones are released. At the same time, your brain creates healthy neural pathways, which will make it increasingly easier to have a positive perspective in the future. In turn, this positive thinking will shift a limited or fixed mindset to one of abundance and growth. Additionally, practicing generosity and gratitude creates a mindset of abundance by helping you focus on what you have, rather than what you lack.

Let's get real!

Activity:

Please complete the following activity by carefully considering and answering the question below.

1. In what other ways do the GOOD LIFE principles covered in the last five lessons support the idea of financial self-investment?

_____

_____

_____

_____

Investing and Investing in Yourself:

Current investing vs. long-term investing will be covered in more detail in future classes, but I want to introduce the concepts in this class. Let's consider how this concept applies to all areas of self-investment covered in this lesson.

The Superpower of Investing:

The superpower of investing is compound interest. Compound interest occurs when you earn interest on the money that you save *and* the interest that you earn. If something compounds—meaning, a little growth serves as the fuel for future growth—a small starting point can lead to results so extraordinary they seem to defy logic. It can be so logic-defying that you underestimate what's possible (Housel, 2020).

I hope you're already seeing the benefits of investing. Successful investors, like Warren Buffett, have been investing consistently and for a long time. Time and consistency are the key drivers of success. Your money needs time to compound, so the sooner you start, the better off you'll be.

The principle of compounding works based on time, consistency, and interest paid. Your money will double with compounding interest within a period of time based on the interest being paid.

The Rule of 72 helps explain this: It's simple; divide your interest rate by 72 to calculate the time it will take to double your investment. So, if you're earning 10% interest, divide 72 by 10. In this case, it will take 7.2 years to double your investment.

To learn more about The Rule of 72 visit the course resources.

The main takeaway here is that the sooner you start and the longer you stay in, the better results you will achieve with compound interest. There is more involved, but we'll dig into that in future classes.

Benefits of Short- and Long-Term Investing:

1. Compound interest can help you double your money over a span of time based on interest paid.
2. With current or short-term investing, you get to experience the results of compounding interest while you wait for the results

of your long-term investments. This builds your confidence in investing.

We'll come back to these benefits after covering the other self-investment areas.

Physical Self-Investment:

Maintain a healthy body by getting proper rest, eating nutritious foods, and exercising. Additionally, avoid harmful habits and make sure to schedule annual checkups with your physician.

Remember, you're worth it! You can't put a price tag on your health. All the money in the world is not worth neglecting your health.

Let's get real!

Activity:

Please complete the following activity by carefully considering and answering the question below.

1. How do the GOOD LIFE principles covered in the last five lessons offer opportunities for or support the idea of physical self-investment?

_____

_____

_____

_____

_____

Emotional Self-Investment:

Emotional self-investment involves developing and practicing emotional intelligence. This will help you to appropriately express your emotions, to adjust to change, to cope with stress in healthy ways, and to enjoy life, despite its occasional disappointments and frustrations.

It also means developing the ability to address problems or conflicts in appropriate and constructive manners.

Let's get real!

Activity:

Please complete the following activity by carefully considering and answering the question below.

1. How do GOOD LIFE principles covered in the last five lessons offer opportunities for or support the idea of emotional self-investment?

_____

_____

_____

_____

Mental Self-Investment:

By developing a mental self-investment regimen, you can help reduce your stress and anxiety, and you can increase your resiliency. The mind is the source of all our thoughts, words, and actions, and it is both powerful and capable.

Our brains change as we think—a concept referred to as neuroplasticity—and they grow new brain cells through neurogenesis. Using the powers in our minds, we can persist and grow in response to life's challenges. Through mental self-investment we can improve the way we think and how we live.

Let's get real!

Activity:

Please complete the following activity by carefully considering and answering the question below.

1. How do GOOD LIFE principles covered in the last five lessons offer opportunities for or support the idea of mental self-investment?

_____

_____

_____

_____

Spiritual Self-Investment:

Spiritual self-investment comes with several benefits, including a better mood, less anxiety and depression, and even fewer aches and illnesses.

For many people, spirituality means observing rituals, studying texts, and attending religious services. For others, it's not at all about traditional strictures or notions of God. Spirituality can provide the sense that life is meaningful and has a purpose, and it provides a personal framework for the ethics, values, and morals that guide and give meaning and direction to life.

Let's get real!

Activity:

Please complete the following activity by carefully considering and answering the question below.

1. How do GOOD LIFE principles covered in the last five lessons offer opportunities for or support the idea of spiritual self-investment and why?

_____

_____

_____

_____

_____

Occupational Self-Investment:

Practicing occupational self-investment will help you to maintain, develop, and use your gifts, skills, and talents to make an impact on the world. In turn, this will help you to gain personal enrichment, a sense of purpose, and happiness in your life.

Activity:

Please complete the following activity by carefully considering and answering the question below.

1. How do GOOD LIFE principles covered in the last five lessons offer opportunities for or support the idea of occupational self-investment and why?

_____

_____

_____

_____

_____

Financial Health + Physical Health + Emotional Health + Mental Health + Spiritual Health + Occupational Health = Wellness

Self-Investment with Compound Interest

We can take lessons from the power of compounding and the keys of time and consistency to teach us about maximizing other areas of self-investment.

Let's recall the explanation of compound interest: Compound interest is when you earn interest on the money you originally saved as well as the interest you earn on that money, and it can have results that defy logic.

So, imagine the compounding effect of consistently investing in yourself in each of these areas. The compounding effect can be described as the growth that happens in your mindset as you consistently practice new behaviors, new ways of thinking, and new attitudes for a period ranging from 61 days to many years. The following activity will help you connect the idea of compound interest to the idea of self-investment.

Let's get real!

Activity:

Please complete the following activity by filling in the spaces below.

List the five areas of self-investment.

1. _____
2. _____
3. _____
4. _____
5. _____

Activity:

Please complete each of the following exercises by following the steps and answering the questions.

Financial Self-Investment Exercise

1. Close your eyes and visualize what the starting point of financial self-investment looks like for you? What would be the immediate benefits of financial self-investment?

_____

_____

_____

_____

_____

2. Now visualize what 5 years of consistent financial self-investment looks like and write your thoughts down?

_____

_____

_____

_____

3. Resist the urge to underestimate what's possible and visualize the extraordinary and logic-defying results financial self-investment could lead to. Write down what you see.

_____

_____

_____

_____

Physical Self-Investment Exercise

1. Close your eyes and visualize what the starting point of physical self-investment looks like for you? What would be the immediate benefits of physical self-investment?

_____

_____

_____

_____

2. Now visualize what 5 years of consistent physical self-investment looks like and write your thoughts down?

_____

_____

_____

_____

_____

3. Resist the urge to underestimate what's possible and visualize the extraordinary and logic-defying results physical self-investment could lead to. Write down what you see.

_____

_____

_____

_____

_____

Emotional Self-Investment Exercise

1. Close your eyes and visualize what the starting point of emotional self-investment looks like for you? What would be the immediate benefits of emotional self-investment?

_____

_____

_____

_____

_____

2. Now visualize what 5 years of consistent emotional self-investment looks like and write your thoughts down?

_____

_____

_____

_____

3. Resist the urge to underestimate what's possible and visualize the extraordinary and logic-defying results emotional self-investment could lead to. Write down what you see.

_____

_____

_____

_____

Mental Self-Investment Exercise

1. Close your eyes and visualize what the starting point of mental self-investment looks like for you? What would be the immediate benefits of mental self-investment?

_____

_____

_____

_____

2. Now visualize what 5 years of consistent mental self-investment looks like and write your thoughts down?

_____

_____

_____

_____

_____

3. Resist the urge to underestimate what's possible and visualize the extraordinary and logic-defying results mental self-investment could lead to. Write down what you see.

_____

_____

_____

_____

_____

Spiritual Self-Investment Exercise

1. Close your eyes and visualize what the starting point of spiritual self-investment looks like for you? What would be the immediate benefits of spiritual self-investment?

_____

_____

_____

_____

_____

2. Now visualize what 5 years of consistent spiritual self-investment looks like and write your thoughts down?

_____

_____

_____

_____

3. Resist the urge to underestimate what's possible and visualize the extraordinary and logic-defying results spiritual self-investment could lead to. Write down what you see.

_____

_____

_____

_____

Reflective Activity:

Please complete the following reflective activity by sharing your thoughts below.

1. Take a few minutes to journal about the self-investment area that you feel you are strongest in and why.

_____

_____

_____

_____

2. Now, journal about the self-investment area in which you need the most improvement, and why.

_____

_____

_____

_____

_____

Summary:

The six areas of self-investment are: financial, emotional, mental, physical, spiritual, and occupational.

When you invest in each of these facets, they work synergistically, creating wellness in your life that helps propel you forward to achieve your life goals and to live your version of the good life.

Lesson Recap:

1. In this lesson I was able to: (check all that apply)

    ☐ Assess the various types of self-investment.

    ☐ Explain the benefits of both current & long-term investments.

    ☐ Recall the value of investing in myself.

    ☐ Assess the (first 5) GOOD LIFE principles for self-investment opportunities.

2. How do you feel about this course after this lesson? Do you feel confident in self-investment, as we've discussed it in this lesson? Why or why not?

    _____

    _____

    _____

    _____

3. What is something you appreciated about this lesson? What would you change? Do you have feedback for the instructor?

    _____

    _____

    _____

    _____

Lesson 7

Financial Freedom

Lesson Introduction and Objectives

You are almost through the course! You are doing a great job!

In the last lesson, we looked at self-investment, which included shifting your mindset to view financial self-investments as gifts to yourself rather than as forced duties. This perspective is freeing and empowering. We also examined compound interest and how this concept can be applied to all areas of self-investment. In this lesson we are going to examine the path to financial freedom.

In this lesson, you will:

1. Describe and compare new and old ideologies about financial freedom.
2. Name new strategies for financial freedom.
3. Practice at least one strategy for financial freedom.

Financial Freedom

What does Financial Freedom mean to you?

A widely accepted definition of financial freedom is when passive or investment income exceeds expenses. This is usually the point at which people retire. I refer to that definition as *financial independence*.

Financial independence is important and will be discussed in detail in future Good Life Money Coach Classes.

For now, I would like us to look at financial freedom as a mindset that allows you to enjoy life while you work toward the long-term goals of retirement and financial independence. Whether that comes in ten, twenty, thirty, or more years, it is possible to enjoy GOOD LIFE Financial Freedom today!

Financial freedom, for this purpose, includes freedom from debt, but more importantly, it is about gaining control over your life. It involves developing a mindset that is free from behaviors and patterns such as:

- Imposter syndrome — Believing the lie that you are not enough and that others see you as a fraud is an obstacle to your success.

- Social comparison — Spending your money to impress people who don't care or who don't matter is a financial trap.

- Discontent — Never believing that you have enough is a vicious cycle that will spiral out of control financially and emotionally.

- Worry — Worrying solves nothing; it is a false sense of caring about situations and people, and it leads to anxiety, stress, and fear-based financial decisions.

In order to gain control of your money, you must first gain control of self-defeating behaviors by reprogramming your mindset. Some of the categorical behaviors of the GOOD LIFE Money Mindset are generosity, gratitude, and discipline.

Research shows that proactive behaviors promote good practices. If you can make a conscious effort to practice these behaviors, you will see incredible growth in your mindset, enabling you to gain control of your money and, therefore, to experience more financial freedom.

Enjoy the lesson!

> *Financial Freedom is a mindset that allows you to enjoy life while you work toward your financial goals.*

In the book, **The Psychology of Money**, author Morgan Housel references research by psychologist Angus Campbell. Campbell found that the most powerful common denominator of happiness was having a strong sense of controlling one's life.

Money's greatest intrinsic value—and this cannot be overstated—is its ability to give you control over your time. This does not mean you need to be a millionaire to experience financial freedom, rather it requires control over your spending.

Here are some examples of what financial freedom may look like at different income levels:

- The ability for to take a few days off work when you're sick without falling behind on bills.

- The ability to wait for a better job or contract to come around, rather than having to take the first one you find.

- The ability to have 6 months in your emergency savings account as insulation from financial ruin in the event of a health crisis or job loss.

- The ability to make a career change with lower pay but flexible hours and a remote work option to spend more time with your loved ones.

Using your money to buy time and options has a lifetime benefit that few luxury goods can compete with.

Activity:

Please read the following instructions and complete the activity below.

Basic generally refers to the essentials or the fundamentals. However, for the sake of this exercise, I am turning this term on its ear and borrowing from the slang version of basic: characterizing someone or something as unoriginal, unexceptional, and mainstream. For this activity, we will use the slang definition of basic to consider the differences between basic thinking and GOOD LIFE thinking.

Read the table below to see examples of the differences between basic thinking and GOOD LIFE thinking. Once you have examined the table, complete the empty cells with examples of your own.

Basic Thinking Examples	GOOD LIFE Thinking Examples
Fixed Mindset	Growth Mindset
Accept limiting or scarcity beliefs about money	Embrace abundant beliefs about money
"I'll always have bills, so why try!"	"I have more than enough for needs and wants."
"Money doesn't grow on trees."	"Money comes easily to me, and my wealth multiplies."
"If I don't loan her the money, who will?"	"I am responsible for my needs and my true loved ones will understand."
"I can't trust myself to make smart financial decisions."	"I am ending the cycle of poor financial decisions, so I can live the life I always imagined."

Reflective Activity:

Please complete the following Reflective Activity by following the instructions below.

1. In this lesson you have learned that financial freedom is about enjoying life now by overcoming self-defeating behaviors, such as negative beliefs about money. Take five minutes to list some of the negative beliefs you have about money and prosperity:

_____

_____

_____

_____

_____

_____

_____

_____

_____

_____

_____

Summary:

We defined financial freedom as the mindset that lets you enjoy life while you work toward retirement and financial independence, or the point at which passive income and investments exceed your expenses.

A mindset of financial freedom excludes behaviors and patterns such as imposter syndrome, social comparison, discontent, and worry, and it promotes financially proactive behaviors. Financial freedom can manifest as the ability to take a few days off from work without having to worry about money or as the ability to take a lower paying job with flexible hours, so you can spend more time with your loved ones.

Lesson Recap:

1. In this lesson I was able to: (check all that apply)

    □ Describe and compare new and old ideologies about financial freedom.
    □ Name new strategies for financial freedom.
    □ Practice at least one strategy for financial freedom.

2. How do you feel about this course after this lesson? Do you feel confident in practicing one of the strategies for financial freedom? Why or why not?

_____

_____

_____

_____

_____

3. What is something you appreciated about this lesson? What would you change? Do you have feedback for the instructor?

_____

_____

_____

_____

_____

Lesson 8

Examine the Good Life Stealers in Your Life

Lesson Introduction and Objectives

You have now completed the first seven lessons, and you are onto the final lesson of the class. Congratulations! Give yourself a pat on the back or do a little victory dance! In the previous lesson we discovered strategies for financial freedom, and in this lesson, we will examine the obstacles that prevent you from living the good life.

In this lesson you will:

1. Identify behaviors and mindsets that are not aligned with your values.

2. Practice strategies to help you create positive habits and mindsets as a foundation for financial success.

3. Develop a GOOD LIFE Behaviors Practice Plan ™.

Good Life Stealers

As you have completed each of the lessons to this point, you have learned new attitudes and behaviors to continue practicing. You've also been able to observe and identify other attitudes and behaviors that you no longer want in your life as you develop your Good Life Mindset.

In this lesson, we will bring the good life stealers we have discussed together in one place. We will also revisit the strategies and tips you have learned. Then, we will work together to create a GOOD LIFE Behavior Practice Plan, so you can continue practicing these new behaviors and continue developing the mindset you need to achieve your financial goals and improve your overall wellbeing.

The GOOD LIFE Behaviors Practice Plan is based on multiple neuroscience studies, which show that it takes 61 days to form a new habit.

Let's get real!

Activity:

Please complete the following activity by reading the instructions and completing the chart below.

Recall the first seven GOOD LIFE principles:

- Gratitude/Generosity
- Open Up to Accountability
- Operate According to a Detailed Financial Plan
- Discipline as a Way of Life
- Learn for a Lifetime
- Invest in Yourself
- Financial Freedom

The following chart represents the GOOD LIFE Behaviors Practice Plan. Use the chart as a guide to customize your own GOOD LIFE Behaviors Practice Plan.

GOOD LIFE Principles/ Lesson#	GOOD LIFE Stealers	Acknowledgement Statement	What have you learned about this Good Life Stealer?	What Strategies have you learned during the class to change these behaviors?
Gratitude/ Generosity				
Open Up to Accountability				
Operate According to Detailed Financial Plan				
Discipline as a Way of Life				
Learn for a Lifetime				
Invest in Yourself				
Financial Freedom				
Examine the Good Life Stealers in Your Life				

Reflective Activity:

Please complete the following reflective activity by sharing your thoughts below.

1. What is the most important thing you have learned in the course, and why?

_____

_____

_____

_____

Summary:

The final principle in the GOOD LIFE acrostic is to examine the good life stealers in your life. Throughout the course, we learned about many obstacles that may prevent us from living our versions of the good life, such as negative perspectives and irresponsible behaviors.

Hopefully you have completed or are working on completing your GOOD LIFE Behaviors Practice Plan, which will help you to not only identify the good life stealers in your life but also to overcome them, so you can live your good life!

Lesson Recap:

1. In this lesson I was able to: (check all that apply)

   ☐ Identify behaviors and mindsets that are not aligned with my values.

   ☐ Practice strategies to help create positive habits and mindsets for financial success.

   ☐ Develop a GOOD LIFE Behaviors Practice Plan.

2. How do you feel about this course after this lesson? Do you feel confident in identifying threats to achieving the good life? Why or why not?

_____

_____

_____

_____

3. What is something you appreciated about this lesson? What would you change? Do you have feedback for the instructor?

_____

_____

_____

_____

Final Thoughts

I hope you have enjoyed the first Good Life Money Coach™ Class, *The Good Life Money Mindset: 8 Principles for Living the Good Life Now!*

By this point, you have learned how behavior dictates how you handle your finances and how to master your behavior. You now have the power to live the GOOD LIFE!

Each of the lessons and activities have helped you to actively notice your mindsets and beliefs. I have asked you to consider prior conditioning to help you become more aware of the good life stealers that may jeopardize the realization of your financial goals. I worked to help you shift your mindset by introducing you to new behaviors, attitudes, and habits that can produce the results you want.

It has been a pleasure being your instructor, and I look forward to seeing you in future Good Life Money Coach™ Classes, where we will continue to build upon GOOD LIFE principles as we dive into money management skills, strategies, and knowledge.

It's your life, make it good!™

Final Thoughts

Additional Reading

As someone with a formal education in finance, I have actively sought out books, research papers, and articles to delve deeper into the fascinating interplay of sciences like behavioral science and neuroscience with the realm of personal finance. These readings have been instrumental in enhancing my expertise, allowing me to navigate and leverage the intricate connections between these fields, and apply their insights effectively in my own life, as well as in my work with clients. A few key references are listed below.

Brown, Brené. Daring Greatly: How the Courage to Be Vulnerable Transforms the Way We Live, Love, Parent, and Lead", Gotham Books 2012

Dweck, Carol. "Mindset: The New Psychology of Success", Random House, 2006.

Housel, Morgan. " The Psychology of Money", Harriman House, 2020.

Leaf, Caroline. "Switch On Your Brain", Baker Books, 2013

Murphy, Joseph. "The Power of Your Subconscious Mind. Prentice Hall, 1963.

Pert, C. B. "Molecules of Emotion: The Science Behind Mind-Body Medicine', Simon & Schuster.

Made in the USA
Middletown, DE
26 August 2024